Food: What the Heck

Should I Eat? Cookbook

By

Jonathan Wise

Claim Your Free Gift Now

As a way of saying "thank you" for your purchase, we're offering you a free bonus that's *exclusive* for our book readers.

5 Bonus Instant What the Heck Should I Eat Recipes!

Go to the link below before it expires!

http://www.easysummaries.com/whsierecipes

Food: What the Heck Should I Eat?

Contents

Chicken Kale Salad

Pork Cucumber Salad

Turkey Greens Salad

Mutton Apple Beet Salad

Prawns Fruit Spinach Salad

Food: What the Heck Should I Eat Cookbook

POULTRY RECIPES

Lemony Chicken Potatoes

Turkey and Carrots Stew

Spicy Chicken Spinach

Turkey with Mixed Veggies

Chicken Succotash

Turkey with Broccoli

Food: What the Heck Should I Eat Cookbook

MEAT RECIPES

Beef Tomato Sauce Spinach

Minced Mutton Okra

Beef with Cauliflower

Mutton Green Beans

Beef with Kale and Carrots

Mutton Vegetables Casserole

Food: What the Heck Should I Eat Cookbook: GROCERY LIST

Chicken Tomato Soup

Pumpkin Tomato Turkey Soup

Beef Broccoli Soup

Mutton Cauliflower Soup

Spinach Pork Soup

Salmon Veggie Noodle Soup

Beef Brussels Sprout Salad

Chicken Kale Salad

Pork Cucumber Salad

Turkey Greens Salad

Mutton Apple Beet Salad

Prawns Fruit Spinach Salad

Lemony Chicken Potatoes

Turkey and Carrots Stew

Spicy Chicken Spinach

Turkey with Mixed Veggies

Chicken Succotash

Turkey with Broccoli

Beef Tomato Sauce Spinach

Minced Mutton Okra

Beef with Cauliflower

Mutton Green Beans

Beef with Kale and Carrots

Mutton Vegetables Casserole

Food: What the Heck Should I Eat Cookbook Conclusion:

Claim Your Free Gift Now

FINAL SURPRISE BONUS

Food: What the Heck Should I Eat Cookbook

Introduction:

In the present times, it is hard to keep your health and diet recommendations balanced. The pros and cons of different food items are too volatile for the users. Consider plant related foods, some nutritionists will lobby that their too much intake will cause you health issues, others will say that without their intake your health is going to worsen.

All this confusion leads to a certain question, "what the heck should I eat?" The answer to this question is given by Dr. Hyman in his book called "Food: What the heck should I eat?" He is the Director of a clinic center for functional medicine in

Cleveland. In addition, he is second on the list for Advice, How-To and Miscellaneous category of New York Times Best Sellers. The author has presented a clear and easy to understand insight with scientific backing reasons for what sort of food a person should consume depending on the user.

Food: What the Heck Should I Eat Cookbook

What causes food confusion?

The main theme of the book is based on the fact that most food related information doesn't have any authentic sourcing and is more of a misinformation. Hyman lay emphasis that the assumed information must be studied scientifically and proved before propagating it as during the course of nutritional history it has been done very rarely.

It is not easy to judge and study the effects of diet changes in a person without physically examining him and his lifestyle. Suppose a person who initiates a diet having kale, he also can stop going to the gym or even start smoking alongside it. This hardens the effect of kale on the betterment of his health. The author also ponders that it's not necessary that policies will be based on scientific reasoning despite that it should be. He pointed out the lobbying done by large agricultural businesses may be against science and rather to boost their wealth, they might work on spreading misinformation.

The American Congress formed The National Academy of Sciences for reviewing guidelines for different items and it was revealed that the industry was highly influential on the guideline processes and important data was ignored to be assessed. This made it clear that large firms and businesses do affect the policies and spread disinformation.

Consider coconut oil, it was debated to be threatening to human health in 2017 on the basis of a review by the American Heart Association. According the author, the review was devised on the basis of an old approach that saturated fat was highly linked to cause heart diseases.

To avoid all this confusion and misinformation, Hyman has written his masterpiece to allow the reader to have a better insight into nutrition and diet plan choosing.

Food: What the Heck Should I Eat Cookbook

"What The Heck Should We Eat?"

The book filters out large chunks of dietary science and information apart. It is very easy to understand and the reason for it is the organization of the content of the book.

The book is divided in different sections based on different food groups like meat, fruits, poultry, beverages and poultry etc. In the beginning of every chapter, there is an "IQ Quiz" about nutrition. This quiz sets aside every ambiguity about nutrition.

Further ahead, the author then explained where the agenda of policy makers and scientists was correct and where it was wrong. He does it on the basis of different scientific facts and studies. This helps a lot in cross checking the popular beliefs in even the most nutrition informed food lovers. Considering the chicken chapter, the author explains why it is unnecessary and of no use to put "hormone free" stickers on chickens as it is illegal to feed hormones to poultry in the US. In the dairy portion, he refers that it is pointless to add fat-soluble Vitamin D and A again to fat-less milk, the reason he gave is that fat plays an important factor to digest these vitamins.

The author proficiently ponders those domains which other major organizations or people ignore. Fruit has been presently referred to be very sugary by media these days and portray it as harmful for health, contrary to that some people believe that its antioxidant functions and fiber as the most beneficial food. Hyman uses an approach which is based on realities and facts rather than pretentious science which has spread misinformation. He deeply examines and studies the anti-oxidant function of fruit and the criticality of fiber while fructose consumption. He also ponders the grounds to support the differentiation between food and vegetables.

At the end of every chapter, there is a reference list about different elements of different foods and in how much quantity they should be consumed. It also has a portion of foods with claims about nutrition on its packing which should be avoided, avoiding fishes which fit completely in one pan like sardines and anchovies etc. He also has a portion about opting for odd vegetables which cannot be changed genetically like kohlrabi and purslane.

Food: What the Heck Should I Eat Cookbook

The "Pegan Diet": An Invention by Mark Hyman:

Hyman has summarized his entire conclusions into an easy-to-act-upon solution. It is a diet which is based on the healthiest paelo and vegan diets, which he calls the 'pegan diet'. According to him, the standard vegan diet is based upon plant based foods which are highly rich in minerals, vitamins, fibers, antioxidants, healthy fats and fibers. The diet is very eco-conscious but unable to provide necessary omega-3 fatty acids like EPA & DHA and zinc, iron or copper etc.

An ideal paleo diet abstains from grains, legumes, sugar, beans and includes fish, nuts, seed and non-industrial meat etc. He also ponders that a few people use this diet as an excuse to consume a greater amount of meat and plant-based foods. Both these foods are devised on that it doesn't grow blood sugar, include a lot of fruits and veggies etc.

His diet starts with a coffee in the morning, a rich in vitamins smoothie or a rich in protein combination of eggs raised in pasture with tomato or avocado. He eats a fresh salad for lunch and at dinner he consumes a small quantity of meat with different vegetables. There are recipes which are convenient to prepare by the users and gives out the message that time consumption due to cooking is a vital reason to a healthier lifestyle.

Food: What the Heck Should I Eat Cookbook

SOUP RECIPES

Chicken Tomato Soup

Serves: 5

Prep Time: 8 minutes

Cooking Time: 12 minutes

Total Time: 20 minutes

Ingredients:

- 3 pounds fresh tomatoes, chopped

- 1 pound grass-fed chicken, cooked and shredded

- 1 garlic clove, minced

- 2 teaspoons dried parsley, crushed

- 1 medium onion, chopped

- 2 tablespoons homemade tomato sauce

- 1 tablespoon balsamic vinegar

- 1 tablespoon olive oil

- 2 tablespoons sugar

- 2 teaspoons dried basil, crushed

- 5 cups low-sodium vegetable broth

- ¼ cup fresh basil, chopped

- Salt and freshly ground black pepper, to taste

Directions:

1. Heat the oil in a large skillet and sauté garlic and onion for 3 minutes.

2. Add tomatoes, herbs, tomato sauce, broth, salt and black pepper and stir for 5 minutes.

3. Close the lid and let simmer for 3 minutes on medium-low heat.

4. Stir in the vinegar and sugar and transfer the mixture in the immersion blender.

5. Blend until smooth and stir in chicken.

6. Garnish with basil and serve in soup bowls.

Nutritional Information per Serving:

Calories 257

Total Fat 6.3 g

Saturated Fat 1.3 g

Cholesterol 70 mg

Total Carbs 19 g

Sugar 13.1 g

Fiber 3.9 g

Sodium 159 mg

Potassium 855 mg

Protein 31 g

Pumpkin Tomato Turkey Soup

Serves: 4

Prep Time: 15 minutes

Cooking Time: 20 minutes

Total Time: 35 minutes

Ingredients:

- 1 pound grass-fed turkey, chunked

- 1 cup tomatoes, chopped

- 4 tablespoons butter

- 1 potato, roughly diced

- 3 tablespoons sun dried tomatoes

- 1 onion, roughly sliced

- 3 tablespoons tomato paste

- 2 teaspoons salt

- 2 pinches black pepper

- 4 tablespoons pumpkin puree

- 1 carrot, roughly chopped

- 4 cups water

- 1 teaspoon pumpkin spice powder

Directions:

1. Heat the butter in a large skillet and add carrots and onions.

2. Sauté for 4 minutes and add turkey meat.

3. Cook for 5 minutes and add tomatoes, tomato paste, potatoes, pumpkin puree, water, sun dried tomatoes, salt and black pepper.

4. Close the lid and let it simmer for 10 minutes on medium-low heat.

5. Take out the turkey meat and transfer the mixture to an immersion blender.

6. Blend until smooth and put the meat back into the soup.

7. Sprinkle pumpkin spice powder and serve hot in soup bowls.

Nutritional Information per Serving:

Calories 405

Total Fat 26.3 g

Saturated Fat 12.2 g

Cholesterol 38 mg

Total Carbs 19.6 g

Sugar 7 g

Fiber 3.7 g

Sodium 1364 mg

Potassium 615 mg

Protein 25.5 g

Beef Broccoli Soup

Serves: 4

Prep Time: 8 minutes

Cooking Time: 12 minutes

Total Time: 20 minutes

Ingredients:

- 1 pound grass-fed beef, boiled and shredded

- 1 cup broccoli florets, washed and blanched

- 1 tablespoon celery leaves, chopped

- 2 garlic cloves, minced

- 2 tablespoons vegetable oil

- 1 small onion, chopped

- 4 cups vegetable stock

- ½ cup full fat milk

- 1 teaspoon salt

- 1 teaspoon freshly ground black pepper

Directions:

1. Heat the oil in a large skillet and add celery, garlic and onions.

2. Sauté for 3 minutes and add broccoli florets, vegetable stock, salt and black pepper.

3. Cook for 5 minutes and transfer the mixture in the blender.

4. Add milk and blend until smooth.

5. Put back in the skillet and add beef.

6. Let simmer for 3 minutes and dish out in small soup bowls to serve steaming hot.

Nutritional Information per Serving:

Calories 299

Total Fat 18.7 g

Saturated Fat 6.2 g

Cholesterol 78 mg

Total Carbs 6.1 g

Sugar 3.3 g

Fiber 1.5 g

Sodium 150 mg

Potassium 126 mg

Protein 25.4 g

Mutton Cauliflower Soup

Serves: 4

Prep Time: 8 minutes

Cooking Time: 12 minutes

Total Time: 20 minutes

Ingredients:

- 1 pound mutton, boiled and shredded

- 3 cups cauliflower florets

- 2 tablespoons olive oil

- 4 cups mutton stock

- 4 potatoes, chopped

- 12 slices of bacon, crisp fried

- 1 large onion, chopped

- 1 tablespoon salt

- 1 tablespoon black pepper

Directions:

1. Heat the olive oil in a large skillet and add onions.

2. Sauté for 4 minutes and add potatoes, mutton stock, cauliflower florets and browned bacon.

3. Cook for 8 minutes and transfer the mixture in the blender.

4. Blend all the ingredients to a smooth paste and put back in the skillet.

5. Add mutton and season with salt and black pepper.

6. Dish out and serve hot.

Nutritional Information per Serving:

Calories 541

Total Fat 22.6 g

Saturated Fat 5.6 g

Cholesterol 104 mg

Total Carbs 42.9 g

Sugar 6.8 g

Fiber 8.2 g

Sodium 853 mg

Potassium 1565 mg

Protein 43 g

Spinach Pork Soup

Serves: 3

Prep Time: 7 minutes

Cooking Time: 13 minutes

Total Time: 20 minutes

Ingredients:

- ½ pound grass-fed pork, boiled and shredded

- 1 cup spinach puree

- 3 tablespoons canola oil

- 1 cup white sauce

- 1 medium onion, roughly sliced

- 1 tablespoon tomato paste

- 3 cups water

- 3 garlic cloves, minced

- 1 tablespoon sun dried tomatoes

- 2 teaspoons salt

- 2 pinches black pepper

Directions:

1. Heat the canola oil in a large skillet and add garlic and onions.

2. Sauté for 3 minutes and add spinach puree, water and tomato paste.

3. Cook for 7 minutes and add white sauce.

4. Transfer the mixture in the immersion blender and blend until smooth.

5. Put the mixture back in the skillet and add pork meat.

6. Simmer for 3 minutes and garnish with sun dried tomatoes.

Nutritional Information per Serving:

Calories 504

Total Fat 41.3 g

Saturated Fat 9.8 g

Cholesterol 51 mg

Total Carbs 17.4 g

Sugar 9.7 g

Fiber 1.7 g

Sodium 2301 mg

Potassium 289 mg

Protein 14.2 g

Salmon Veggie Noodle Soup

Serves: 5

Prep Time: 5 minutes

Cooking Time: 10 minutes

Total Time: 15 minutes

Ingredients:

- 1 pound salmon, boiled and chunked

- ½ cup peas

- ½ cup carrots

- 6 oz. noodles, cooked and drained

- ½ cup onions

- 3 garlic cloves, minced

- 1 cup tomatoes, diced

- 1 cup baby carrots

- 5 cups vegetable stock

- 1 tablespoon olive oil

- ½ cup potatoes, diced

- ½ cup cauliflower

- ½ inch ginger, minced

- 2 teaspoons Worcestershire sauce

- 1 teaspoon salt

- 1 teaspoon black pepper

Directions:

1. Heat the olive oil in a large skillet and add carrots, onions, ginger, garlic and cauliflowers in a large skillet.

2. Sauté for 4 minutes and add tomatoes, potatoes, vegetable stock, peas and Worcestershire sauce.

3. Cook for 6 minutes and add cooked noodles and salmon.

Season with salt and black pepper and serve hot.

Nutritional Information per Serving:

Calories 248

Total Fat 9.4 g

Saturated Fat 1.4 g

Cholesterol 50 mg

Total Carbs 20.5 g

Sugar 5.3 g

Fiber 3.8 g

Sodium 142 mg

Potassium 675 mg

Protein 21.6 g

Food: What the Heck Should I Eat Cookbook

SALADS RECIPES

Beef Brussels Sprout Salad

Serves: 4

Prep Time: 5 minutes

Cooking Time: 5 minutes

Total Time: 10 minutes

Ingredients:

- ½ pound beef, boiled and chunked

- 1 pound Brussels sprouts, trimmed and halved

- 1 cup pomegranate seeds

- ½ tablespoon unsalted butter, melted

- ¼ cup cashew nuts, chopped

- ¼ cup almonds, chopped

- 3 cups water

- Salt and black pepper, to taste

Directions:

1. Heat water in a large pot and add Brussels sprouts.

2. Boil for 5 minutes on high heat and dish out in a bowl.

3. Add melted butter, beef chunks, cashew nuts, pomegranate seeds and almonds.

Nutritional Information per Serving:

Calories 276

Total Fat 12.3 g

Saturated Fat 3.4 g

Cholesterol 55 mg

Total Carbs 20.4 g

Sugar 6.1 g

Fiber 5.5 g

Sodium 83 mg

Potassium 763 mg

Protein 23.9 g

Chicken Kale Salad

Serves: 6

Prep Time: 6 hours

Cooking Time: 0 minutes

Total Time: 6 hours

Ingredients:

- 1 pound chicken, boiled and chunked

- 2 fresh tomatoes, sliced

- 2 scallions, chopped

- 3 tablespoon fresh orange juice

- 2 tablespoons almonds, chopped

- 6 cups fresh kale, trimmed and chopped

- 1 red onion, sliced

- 1 tablespoon fresh lemon juice

Directions:

1. Mix together all the ingredients except almonds in a

large bowl.

2. Cover and refrigerate to marinate for around 6

hours.

3. Take out from the refrigerator and stir in almonds

and serve.

Nutritional Information per Serving:

Calories 179

Total Fat 3.4 g

Saturated Fat 0.8 g

Cholesterol 58 mg

Total Carbs 12 g

Sugar 2.8 g

Fiber 2.3 g

Sodium 81 mg

Potassium 641 mg

Protein 25.1 g

Pork Cucumber Salad

Serves: 5

Prep Time: 5 minutes

Cooking Time: 0 minutes

Total Time: 5 minutes

Ingredients:

- 1 pound pork meat, boiled and chunked

- 2 cups cucumber, spiraled with blade C

- 2 cups grape tomatoes, halved

- 1 tablespoon fresh oregano, chopped

- 1 garlic clove, minced

- 2 tablespoons balsamic vinegar

- 1 cup black olives, pitted and halved

- 1 tablespoon fresh basil, chopped

- 2 tablespoons olive oil

- Salt and freshly ground black pepper, to taste

Directions:

1. Mix together all the ingredients in a large serving bowl.

2. Toss to coat well and serve immediately.

Nutritional Information per Serving:

Calories 344

Total Fat 28 g

Saturated Fat 8.5 g

Cholesterol 64 mg

Total Carbs 6.8 g

Sugar 2.7 g

Fiber 2.3 g

Sodium 291 mg

Potassium 257 mg

Protein 16.5 g

Turkey Greens Salad

Serves: 3

Prep Time: 10 minutes

Cooking Time: 0 minutes

Total Time: 10 minutes

Ingredients:

- ½ pound turkey, boiled and chunked

- 1 large green apple, cored and sliced

- 2 tablespoons apple cider vinegar

- 4 cups mixed fresh greens

- 1 tablespoon unsalted cashews

- Salt and freshly ground black pepper, to taste

Directions:

1. Toss together greens, apple and cashews in a large serving bowl except vinegar.

2. Drizzle with apple cider vinegar and serve.

Nutritional Information per Serving:

Calories 307

Total Fat 14.6 g

Saturated Fat 2.8 g

Cholesterol 61 mg

Total Carbs 20.6 g

Sugar 14.6 g

Fiber 3.2 g

Sodium 133 mg

Potassium 328 mg

Protein 25.5 g

Mutton Apple Beet Salad

Serves: 6

Prep Time: 15 minutes

Cooking Time: 0 minutes

Total Time: 15 minutes

Ingredients:

For Salad

- 1 pound grass-fed mutton, boiled and shredded

- 2 cups beetroot, peeled and grated

- 2 cups Braeburn apple, peeled, cored and grated

- 2 cups carrots, peeled and grated

For Dressing

- 1 tablespoon raw honey

- 2 tablespoons olive oil

- 1 tablespoon fresh ginger-root, finely grated

- 3 tablespoons fresh lime juice

Directions:

1. Mix together all the salad ingredients in a large serving bowl.

2. Beat together all the dressing ingredients in another bowl until well-combined

3. Drizzle the dressing over salad and mix thoroughly.

4. Refrigerate before serving.

Nutritional Information per Serving:

Calories 287

Total Fat 12.1 g

Saturated Fat 3.3 g

Cholesterol 70 mg

Total Carbs 23.1 g

Sugar 17.1 g

Fiber 3.9 g

Sodium 127 mg

Potassium 643 mg

Protein 22.8 g

Prawns Fruit Spinach Salad

Serves: 6

Prep Time: 20 minutes

Cooking Time: 0 minutes

Total Time: 20 minutes

Ingredients:

- 1 pound prawns, cooked

- 1 mango, peeled, pitted and cubed

- 2 papayas, peeled, seeded and cubed

- ¼ cup fresh mint leaves, chopped

- 8 cups fresh baby spinach

- 1 pound fresh pineapple, peeled and cut into chunks

- 3 tablespoons fresh lime juice

Directions:

1. Put all the ingredients except spinach in a large serving bowl and mix thoroughly.

2. Cover and refrigerate to chill before serving.

3. Put the spinach in serving plates and top with salad before serving.

Nutritional Information per Serving:

Calories 222

Total Fat 2.1 g

Saturated Fat 0.6 g

Cholesterol 159 mg

Total Carbs 34.4 g

Sugar 23.8 g

Fiber 5 g

Sodium 228 mg

Potassium 762 mg

Protein 20 g

Food: What the Heck Should I Eat Cookbook

POULTRY RECIPES

Lemony Chicken Potatoes

Serves: 4

Prep Time: 5 minutes

Cooking Time: 18 minutes

Total Time: 23 minutes

Ingredients:

- 1 pound grass-fed chicken, bone-in

- 2 tablespoons olive oil

- 2 cups chicken broth

- 3 tablespoons fresh lemon juice

- 3 tablespoons fresh rosemary, chopped

- 8 medium potatoes, scrubbed and cubed

- Salt and freshly ground black pepper, to taste

Directions:

1. Heat olive oil in a skillet and add potatoes.

2. Sauté for 3 minutes and add rosemary, chicken, salt and black pepper.

3. Cook for 3 minutes and add chicken broth.

4. Close the lid and cook for 8 minutes on medium-

low heat and stir in lemon juice.

5. Let it simmer for 3 minutes and serve warm.

Nutritional Information per Serving:

Calories 495

Total Fat 9.6 g

Saturated Fat 1.6 g

Cholesterol 76 mg

Total Carbs 69.2 g

Sugar 5.5 g

Fiber 11.3 g

Sodium 487 mg

Potassium 1875 mg

Protein 36.1 g

Turkey and Carrots Stew

Serves: 3

Prep Time: 5 minutes

Cooking Time: 15 minutes

Total Time: 20 minutes

Ingredients:

- 1 pound grass-fed turkey meat

- ½ cup water

- 1 tablespoon butter

- ½ teaspoon red pepper flakes, crushed

- 1 pound carrots, peeled and sliced diagonally

- ¼ cup golden raisins

- ¼ teaspoon salt

Directions:

1. Heat butter in a skillet and add turkey meat.

2. Cook for 4 minutes and add carrots, raisins and water.

3. Cook for 3 minutes and add golden raisins, salt and red pepper flakes.

4. Cover and cook for 7 minutes on low heat.

5. Dish out and serve hot.

Nutritional Information per Serving:

Calories 420

Total Fat 22.1 g

Saturated Fat 8.5 g

Cholesterol 21 mg

Total Carbs 26.1 g

Sugar 16.1 g

Fiber 4.3 g

Sodium 225 mg

Potassium 581 mg

Protein 31.9 g

Spicy Chicken Spinach

Serves: 3

Prep Time: 10 minutes

Cooking Time: 15 minutes

Total Time: 25 minutes

Ingredients:

- 1 pound grass-fed chicken, boneless

- 12-oz spinach

- 1 inch ginger, chopped

- 2 small onions, thinly sliced

- 6 garlic cloves

- ½ teaspoon turmeric powder

- ½ teaspoon red chili powder

- 1 teaspoon salt

- 1 tablespoon oil

- 1 teaspoon cumin powder

- 2 teaspoons coriander powder

Directions:

1. Put the oil in the Instant Pot and select "Sauté".

2. Add ginger, cumin seeds and garlic and sauté for about 45 seconds.

3. Add onions and sauté for 3 minutes.

4. Put the coriander powder, turmeric powder, spinach, salt and red chili powder.

5. Lock the lid and set the Instant Pot to "Manual" at high pressure for 8 minutes.

6. Release the pressure quickly and dish out the chicken.

7. Put the spinach in an immersion blender and blend well.

8. Transfer the spinach and chicken again in the instant pot and select "Sauté".

9. Let simmer for 3 minutes and dish out.

Nutritional Information per Serving:

Calories 358

Total Fat 18.9 g

Saturated Fat 4.8 g

Cholesterol 95 mg

Total Carbs 11.7 g

Sugar 2.6 g

Fiber 4 g

Sodium 968 mg

Potassium 764 mg

Protein 35.4 g

Turkey with Mixed Veggies

Serves: 4

Prep Time: 5 minutes

Cooking Time: 15 minutes

Total Time: 20 minutes

Ingredients:

- 1 pound grass-fed turkey

- 1 tablespoon olive oil

- 1 bell pepper, diced

- 1 small onion, thinly sliced

- 1 garlic clove, minced

- 1 teaspoon basil

- 1 Japanese eggplant, peeled and sliced

- 1 teaspoon oregano

- 3 tablespoons water

- ¼ teaspoon red pepper flakes

- 1 zucchini, sliced

- 1 medium potato, peeled and diced

- 1 tablespoon tomato paste

- Salt and freshly ground black pepper, to taste

Directions:

1. Heat olive oil in a skillet and add garlic and onions.

2. Sauté for 2 minutes and add potatoes and turkey.

3. Sauté for 3 minutes and add the remaining ingredients.

4. Cover the lid and cook for 10 minutes on medium-low heat.

5. Dish out and serve hot.

Nutritional Information per Serving:

Calories 351

Total Fat 17.7 g

Saturated Fat 5.1 g

Cholesterol 8 mg

Total Carbs 25.3 g

Sugar 9.3 g

Fiber 7.7 g

Sodium 85 mg

Potassium 801 mg

Protein 26.5 g

Chicken Succotash

Serves: 6

Prep Time: 8 minutes

Cooking Time: 12 minutes

Total Time: 20 minutes

Ingredients:

- 1 pound grass-fed chicken, bone-in

- 2 cups complete corn kernels

- 2 cups water

- 2 cups lima beans

- 2 cups tomatoes

- 1 cup bell peppers

- 3 tablespoons butter

- 2 teaspoons salt

Directions:

1. Melt the butter in the pressure cooker and add bell peppers.

2. Sauté for 2 minutes and add rest of the ingredients.

3. Cover the lid and cook for about 10 minutes at high pressure.

4. Release the pressure naturally and dish out to serve hot.

Nutritional Information per Serving:

Calories 282

Total Fat 13.5 g

Saturated Fat 5.8 g

Cholesterol 63 mg

Total Carbs 19.7 g

Sugar 5.4 g

Fiber 4.2 g

Sodium 201 mg

Potassium 425 mg

Protein 20.6 g

Turkey with Broccoli

Serves: 4

Prep Time: 5 minutes

Cooking Time: 13 minutes

Total Time: 18 minutes

Ingredients:

- 1 pound grass-fed turkey, bone-in

- 1 pound broccoli florets

- 2 tablespoons butter, melted

- ½ cup almonds

- 1 cup water

- Salt and freshly ground black pepper, to taste

Directions:

1. Melt the butter in the skillet and add turkey.

2. Cook for 5 minutes and add broccoli florets, water, salt and black pepper.

3. Cover the lid and cook for 8 minutes on medium-low heat.

4. Uncover and stir in almonds and serve hot.

Nutritional Information per Serving:

Calories 374

Total Fat 25.7 g

Saturated Fat 8.6 g

Cholesterol 23 mg

Total Carbs 11.2 g

Sugar 3.6 g

Fiber 4.4 g

Sodium 148 mg

Potassium 448 mg

Protein 28.4 g

Food: What the Heck Should I Eat Cookbook

MEAT RECIPES

Beef Tomato Sauce Spinach

Serves: 5

Prep Time: 5 minutes

Cooking Time: 25 minutes

Total Time: 30 minutes

Ingredients:

- 1 pound grass-fed beef, boneless

- 1 tablespoon olive oil

- 1 teaspoon garlic, minced

- 5 cups fresh spinach, chopped

- ½ cup tomatoes, chopped

- 1 small onion, chopped

- ½ teaspoon red pepper flakes, crushed

- ¼ cup homemade tomato puree

- ½ cup vegetable broth

- ¼ cup white wine

Directions:

1. Heat olive oil in a skillet and add onions.

2. Sauté for 3 minutes and add spinach, garlic and red pepper flakes.

3. Cook for 4 minutes and add beef and rest of the ingredients.

4. Cover the lid and cook for 18 minutes.

5. Open the lid and dish out to serve hot.

Nutritional Information per Serving:

Calories 218

Total Fat 12 g

Saturated Fat 4.1 g

Cholesterol 60 mg

Total Carbs 4.4 g

Sugar 1.8 g

Fiber 1.4 g

Sodium 164 mg

Potassium 269 mg

Protein 20.3 g

Minced Mutton Okra

Serves: 6

Prep Time: 10 minutes

Cooking Time: 20 minutes

Total Time: 30 minutes

Ingredients:

- 3 pounds okra, chopped

- 1½ pounds grass-fed mutton, minced

- 4 tablespoons olive oil

- 2 small onions

- 2 tomatoes

- 1 cup tomato sauce

- 1 teaspoon turmeric powder

- 1 teaspoon garlic powder

- 1 teaspoon cayenne pepper

- 1 teaspoon ginger powder

- 1 teaspoon cumin seeds

- 1 teaspoon coriander powder

- Salt and freshly ground black pepper, to taste

Directions:

1. Stir fry the okra in 2 tablespoons olive oil for 5 minutes and set aside.

2. Heat olive oil in a skillet and add onions and garlic.

3. Sauté for 3 minutes and add tomatoes, turmeric powder, garlic powder, cayenne pepper, ginger powder, cumin seeds, coriander powder, salt and black pepper.

4. Cook for 2 minutes and add minced meat.

5. Cover the lid and cook for 8 minutes.

6. Add fried okra and cook for 3 minutes.

7. Dish out and serve hot.

Nutritional Information per Serving:

Calories 437

Total Fat 20.9 g

Saturated Fat 5.3 g

Cholesterol 104 mg

Total Carbs 24 g

Sugar 7.3 g

Fiber 9.2 g

Sodium 320 mg

Potassium 1366 mg

Protein 37.8 g

Beef with Cauliflower

Serves: 4

Prep Time: 8 minutes

Cooking Time: 17 minutes

Total Time: 25 minutes

Ingredients:

- 1 pound grass-fed beef, boneless

- 1 pound cauliflower

- 1 tablespoon olive oil

- 1 tablespoon fresh lemon juice

- ½ cup vegetable broth

- 1 teaspoon red pepper flakes, crushed

- Salt, to taste

Directions:

1. Season the cauliflower with salt and red pepper flakes.

2. Heat olive oil in a skillet and add beef.

3. Cook for 10 minutes and add cauliflower, vegetable broth, red pepper flakes and salt.

4. Cover the lid and cook for 7 minutes.

5. Stir in the lemon juice and dish out to serve hot.

Nutritional Information per Serving:

Calories 266

Total Fat 14.9 g

Saturated Fat 5.1 g

Cholesterol 75 mg

Total Carbs 6.5 g

Sugar 2.9 g

Fiber 3 g

Sodium 206 mg

Potassium 383 mg

Protein 26 g

Mutton Green Beans

Serves: 4

Prep Time: 15 minutes

Cooking Time: 6 hours

Total Time: 6 hours 15 minutes

Ingredients:

- 1 pound grass-fed mutton

- 2 garlic cloves, minced

- 3 cups water

- 2 pounds fresh green beans

- 3 tablespoons olive oil

- Salt and freshly ground black pepper, to taste

Directions:

1. Heat oil in a crock-pot and add garlic and mutton.

2. Stir gently and add rest of the ingredients.

3. Close the lid and set the crock-pot on low for 6 hours.

4. Open the lid after 6 hours and dish out to serve hot.

Nutritional Information per Serving:

Calories 396

Total Fat 21.6 g

Saturated Fat 5.4 g

Cholesterol 104 mg

Total Carbs 16.7 g

Sugar 3.2 g

Fiber 7.7 g

Sodium 105 mg

Potassium 872 mg

Protein 36.2 g

Beef with Kale and Carrots

Serves: 5

Prep Time: 5 minutes

Cooking Time: 22 minutes

Total Time: 27 minutes

Ingredients:

- 1 pound grass-fed beef

- 3 medium carrots, peeled and cut into ½-inch slices

- 5 garlic cloves, minced

- 2 tablespoons olive oil

- ½ cup beef broth

- 1 tablespoon fresh lemon juice

- 1 cup fresh kale, trimmed and chopped

- 1 small onion, chopped

- ¼ teaspoon red pepper flakes, crushed

- Salt and freshly ground black pepper, to taste

Directions:

1. Put the olive oil, garlic and onions in the pressure cooker.

2. Sauté for 3 minutes and add carrots and beef.

3. Sauté for 4 minutes and add kale, beef broth, red pepper flakes, salt and black pepper.

4. Close the lid and cook for 15 minutes at high pressure.

5. Release the pressure naturally and stir in the lemon juice.

6. Dish out and serve hot with brown rice.

Nutritional Information per Serving:

Calories 245

Total Fat 14.6 g

Saturated Fat 4.5 g

Cholesterol 60 mg

Total Carbs 7.5 g

Sugar 2.6 g

Fiber 1.5 g

Sodium 169 mg

Potassium 241 mg

Protein 20 g

Mutton Vegetables Casserole

Serves: 5

Prep Time: 10 minutes

Cooking Time: 35 minutes

Total Time: 45 minutes

Ingredients:

- 1 pound grass-fed mutton

- 2 cups tomatoes, chopped

- 1 tablespoon olive oil

- ½ cup water

- 16 large eggs

- 1 cup almond flour

- 2 medium green bell peppers, seeded and chopped

- 2 medium zucchinis, chopped

- 1 cup almond milk

- Salt and freshly ground black pepper, to taste

Directions:

1. Heat the olive oil in a pot and add mutton and water.

2. Cover the lid and cook for 10 minutes.

3. Dish out and keep aside.

4. Preheat the oven to 375 degrees F and grease a baking dish.

5. Mix together eggs, almond milk, almond flour, salt and black pepper in a bowl.

6. Beat well and add vegetables and mutton.

7. Transfer the mixture into a baking dish and place the dish in the oven.

8. Bake for 25 minutes and remove from the oven.

9. Serve hot with your favorite dip.

Nutritional Information per Serving:

Calories 592

Total Fat 38.6 g

Saturated Fat 18.8 g

Cholesterol 679 mg

Total Carbs 12.8 g

Sugar 9.2 g

Fiber 3.4 g

Sodium 317 mg

Potassium 1125 mg

Protein 48.9 g

Food: What the Heck Should I Eat Cookbook: GROCERY LIST

Chicken Tomato Soup

Ingredients:

- 3 pounds fresh tomatoes, chopped

- 1 pound grass-fed chicken, cooked and shredded

- 1 garlic clove, minced

- 2 teaspoons dried parsley, crushed

- 1 medium onion, chopped

- 2 tablespoons homemade tomato sauce

- 1 tablespoon balsamic vinegar

- 1 tablespoon olive oil

- 2 tablespoons sugar

- 2 teaspoons dried basil, crushed

- 5 cups low-sodium vegetable broth

- ¼ cup fresh basil, chopped

- Salt and freshly ground black pepper, to taste

Pumpkin Tomato Turkey Soup

Ingredients:

- 1 pound grass-fed turkey, chunked

- 1 cup tomatoes, chopped

- 4 tablespoons butter

- 1 potato, roughly diced

- 3 tablespoons sun dried tomatoes

- 1 onion, roughly sliced

- 3 tablespoons tomato paste

- 2 teaspoons salt

- 2 pinches black pepper

- 4 tablespoons pumpkin puree

- 1 carrot, roughly chopped

- 4 cups water

- 1 teaspoon pumpkin spice powder

Beef Broccoli Soup

Ingredients:

- 1 pound grass-fed beef, boiled and shredded

- 1 cup broccoli florets, washed and blanched

- 1 tablespoon celery leaves, chopped

- 2 garlic cloves, minced

- 2 tablespoons vegetable oil

- 1 small onion, chopped

- 4 cups vegetable stock

- ½ cup full fat milk

- 1 teaspoon salt

- 1 teaspoon freshly ground black pepper

Mutton Cauliflower Soup

Ingredients:

- 1 pound mutton, boiled and shredded

- 3 cups cauliflower florets

- 2 tablespoons olive oil

- 4 cups mutton stock

- 4 potatoes, chopped

- 12 slices of bacon, crisp fried

- 1 large onion, chopped

- 1 tablespoon salt

- 1 tablespoon black pepper

Spinach Pork Soup

Ingredients:

- ½ pound grass-fed pork, boiled and shredded

- 1 cup spinach puree

- 3 tablespoons canola oil

- 1 cup white sauce

- 1 medium onion, roughly sliced

- 1 tablespoon tomato paste

- 3 cups water

- 3 garlic cloves, minced

- 1 tablespoon sun dried tomatoes

- 2 teaspoons salt

- 2 pinches black pepper

Salmon Veggie Noodle Soup

Ingredients:

- 1 pound salmon, boiled and chunked

- ½ cup peas

- ½ cup carrots

- 6 oz. noodles, cooked and drained

- ½ cup onions

- 3 garlic cloves, minced

- 1 cup tomatoes, diced

- 1 cup baby carrots

- 5 cups vegetable stock

- 1 tablespoon olive oil

- ½ cup potatoes, diced

- ½ cup cauliflower

- ½ inch ginger, minced

- 2 teaspoons Worcestershire sauce

- 1 teaspoon salt

- 1 teaspoon black pepper

Beef Brussels Sprout Salad

Ingredients:

- ½ pound beef, boiled and chunked

- 1 pound Brussels sprouts, trimmed and halved

- 1 cup pomegranate seeds

- ½ tablespoon unsalted butter, melted

- ¼ cup cashew nuts, chopped

- ¼ cup almonds, chopped

- 3 cups water

- Salt and black pepper, to taste

Chicken Kale Salad

Ingredients:

- 1 pound chicken, boiled and chunked

- 2 fresh tomatoes, sliced

- 2 scallions, chopped

- 3 tablespoon fresh orange juice

- 2 tablespoons almonds, chopped

- 6 cups fresh kale, trimmed and chopped

- 1 red onion, sliced

- 1 tablespoon fresh lemon juice

Pork Cucumber Salad

Ingredients:

- 1 pound pork meat, boiled and chunked

- 2 cups cucumber, spiraled with blade C

- 2 cups grape tomatoes, halved

- 1 tablespoon fresh oregano, chopped

- 1 garlic clove, minced

- 2 tablespoons balsamic vinegar

- 1 cup black olives, pitted and halved

- 1 tablespoon fresh basil, chopped

- 2 tablespoons olive oil

- Salt and freshly ground black pepper, to taste

Turkey Greens Salad

Ingredients:

- ½ pound turkey, boiled and chunked

- 1 large green apple, cored and sliced

- 2 tablespoons apple cider vinegar

- 4 cups mixed fresh greens

- 1 tablespoon unsalted cashews

- Salt and freshly ground black pepper, to taste

Mutton Apple Beet Salad

Ingredients:

For Salad

- 1 pound grass-fed mutton, boiled and shredded

- 2 cups beetroot, peeled and grated

- 2 cups Braeburn apple, peeled, cored and grated

- 2 cups carrots, peeled and grated

For Dressing

- 1 tablespoon raw honey

- 2 tablespoons olive oil

- 1 tablespoon fresh ginger-root, finely grated

- 3 tablespoons fresh lime juice

Prawns Fruit Spinach Salad

Ingredients:

- 1 pound prawns, cooked

- 1 mango, peeled, pitted and cubed

- 2 papayas, peeled, seeded and cubed

- ¼ cup fresh mint leaves, chopped

- 8 cups fresh baby spinach

- 1 pound fresh pineapple, peeled and cut into chunks

- 3 tablespoons fresh lime juice

Lemony Chicken Potatoes

Ingredients:

- 1 pound grass-fed chicken, bone-in

- 2 tablespoons olive oil

- 2 cups chicken broth

- 3 tablespoons fresh lemon juice

- 3 tablespoons fresh rosemary, chopped

- 8 medium potatoes, scrubbed and cubed

- Salt and freshly ground black pepper, to taste

Turkey and Carrots Stew

Ingredients:

- 1 pound grass-fed turkey meat

- ½ cup water

- 1 tablespoon butter

- ½ teaspoon red pepper flakes, crushed

- 1 pound carrots, peeled and sliced diagonally

- ¼ cup golden raisins

- ¼ teaspoon salt

Spicy Chicken Spinach

Ingredients:

- 1 pound grass-fed chicken, boneless

- 12-oz spinach

- 1 inch ginger, chopped

- 2 small onions, thinly sliced

- 6 garlic cloves

- ½ teaspoon turmeric powder

- ½ teaspoon red chili powder

- 1 teaspoon salt

- 1 tablespoon oil

- 1 teaspoon cumin powder

- 2 teaspoons coriander powder

Turkey with Mixed Veggies

Ingredients:

- 1 pound grass-fed turkey

- 1 tablespoon olive oil

- 1 bell pepper, diced

- 1 small onion, thinly sliced

- 1 garlic clove, minced

- 1 teaspoon basil

- 1 Japanese eggplant, peeled and sliced

- 1 teaspoon oregano

- 3 tablespoons water

- ¼ teaspoon red pepper flakes

- 1 zucchini, sliced

- 1 medium potato, peeled and diced

- 1 tablespoon tomato paste

- Salt and freshly ground black pepper, to taste

Chicken Succotash

Ingredients:

- 1 pound grass-fed chicken, bone-in

- 2 cups complete corn kernels

- 2 cups water

- 2 cups lima beans

- 2 cups tomatoes

- 1 cup bell peppers

- 3 tablespoons butter

- 2 teaspoons salt

Turkey with Broccoli

Ingredients:

- 1 pound grass-fed turkey, bone-in

- 1 pound broccoli florets

- 2 tablespoons butter, melted

- ½ cup almonds

- 1 cup water

- Salt and freshly ground black pepper, to taste

Beef Tomato Sauce Spinach

Ingredients:

- 1 pound grass-fed beef, boneless

- 1 tablespoon olive oil

- 1 teaspoon garlic, minced

- 5 cups fresh spinach, chopped

- ½ cup tomatoes, chopped

- 1 small onion, chopped

- ½ teaspoon red pepper flakes, crushed

- ¼ cup homemade tomato puree

- ½ cup vegetable broth

- ¼ cup white wine

Minced Mutton Okra

Ingredients:

- 3 pounds okra, chopped

- 1½ pounds grass-fed mutton, minced

- 4 tablespoons olive oil

- 2 small onions

- 2 tomatoes

- 1 cup tomato sauce

- 1 teaspoon turmeric powder

- 1 teaspoon garlic powder

- 1 teaspoon cayenne pepper

- 1 teaspoon ginger powder

- 1 teaspoon cumin seeds

- 1 teaspoon coriander powder

- Salt and freshly ground black pepper, to taste

Beef with Cauliflower

Ingredients:

- 1 pound grass-fed beef, boneless

- 1 pound cauliflower

- 1 tablespoon olive oil

- 1 tablespoon fresh lemon juice

- ½ cup vegetable broth

- 1 teaspoon red pepper flakes, crushed

- Salt, to taste

Mutton Green Beans

Ingredients:

- 1 pound grass-fed mutton

- 2 garlic cloves, minced

- 3 cups water

- 2 pounds fresh green beans

- 3 tablespoons olive oil

- Salt and freshly ground black pepper, to taste

Beef with Kale and Carrots

Ingredients:

- 1 pound grass-fed beef

- 3 medium carrots, peeled and cut into ½-inch

  slices

- 5 garlic cloves, minced

- 2 tablespoons olive oil

- ½ cup beef broth

- 1 tablespoon fresh lemon juice

- 1 cup fresh kale, trimmed and chopped

- 1 small onion, chopped

- ¼ teaspoon red pepper flakes, crushed

- Salt and freshly ground black pepper, to taste

Mutton Vegetables Casserole

Ingredients:

- 1 pound grass-fed mutton

- 2 cups tomatoes, chopped

- 1 tablespoon olive oil

- ½ cup water

- 16 large eggs

- 1 cup almond flour

- 2 medium green bell peppers, seeded and chopped

- 2 medium zucchinis, chopped

- 1 cup almond milk

- Salt and freshly ground black pepper, to taste

Food: What the Heck Should I Eat Cookbook Conclusion:

A US based doctor known as Dr. Hyman has written a book called "Food: What the Heck Should I Eat?" In this book, he has given an insight to scientific reasons and grounds for why different types of food group's consumption are necessary for a healthy life style. He argues that industries and large businesses spread false propaganda and misinformation, which leads into confusion for choosing food for common people. The book is divided into different chapters on major categories. He has also cleared many misperceptions about food and where science and policy makers have done wrong. There are recipes and tips for users which help out in tackling misinformation about food spread by different media outlets. The recipes give the message of self-cooking as the key to a healthy lifestyle.

Claim Your Free Gift Now

As a way of saying "thank you" for your purchase, we're offering you a free special bonus that's *exclusive* for our book readers.

5 Bonus Instant What the Heck Should I Eat Recipes!

Go to the link below before it expires!

http://www.easysummaries.com/whsierecip es

FINAL SURPRISE BONUS

Final words from the author…

Hope you enjoyed this book as much as we enjoyed bringing it to you!

I always like to over-deliver, so I'd like to give you one final bonus.

Do me a favor, if you enjoyed this book, please leave a review.

It will help get the word out so more readers can enjoy this book!

If you do, I'll send you one of my most cherished collection – Free:

5 More Tantalizing Recipes on Food: What the Heck Should I Eat? By Jonathan Wise!

Here's how to claim your free report:

1. Leave a review (longer the better but I'd be grateful for whatever length)

2. Send a screenshot of the review here: easysummaries24@gmail.com

3. Receive your bonus within 24-48 hours!

Receive your free bonus – 5 More Tantalizing Recipes on *Food: What the Heck Should I Eat? By Jonathan Wise!* – *immediately*!

CPSIA information can be obtained
at www.ICGtesting.com
Printed in the USA
LVOW11s1509230318
570967LV00001B/228/P